I & II PETER

A MESSAGE FOR TODAY'S CHURCH FROM PETER THE APOSTLE

MIKE MAZZALONGO

BibleTalk.tv

Line by Line Bible Studies

Line by line, verse by verse. These studies are designed to bring out the simple meaning of the biblical text for the modern reader.

Copyright © 2016 by Mike Mazzalongo

ISBN: 978-1-945778-06-3

BibleTalk Books
14998 E. Reno
Choctaw, Oklahoma 73020

Scripture quotations taken from the New American Standard Bible®, Copyright © 1960, 1962, 1963, 1968, 1971, 1972, 1973, 1975, 1977, 1995 by The Lockman Foundation Used by permission. (www.Lockman.org)

TABLE OF CONTENTS

1. THE MEANING OF GRACE: SECURITY   5
2. THE MEANING OF GRACE: SOBRIETY   17
3. THE MEANING OF GRACE: SUBMISSION   27
4. THE MEANING OF GRACE: SUFFERING   39
5. THE MEANING OF GRACE: SERVICE   51
6. PETER'S LAST SERMON   61
7. BEWARE OF FALSE TEACHERS   71
8. DON'T WORRY BE READY   85

4

CHAPTER 1
The Meaning of Grace:
SECURITY

I Peter 1:1-12

Peter the Apostle is a unique biblical character because he had a diverse life for a man of humble origins. There were four important phases in his life:

1. Peter, a successful fisherman

- He lived in Capernaum where Jesus lived as an adult (Mark 1:21).

- He and his brother Andrew had a fishing business together (Matthew 4:18).

- He was married (with children because he served as an elder) (I Peter 5:1).

- His mother-in-law lived with his family (Matthew 8:14).

2. Peter, a disciple of Jesus

Peter knew Jesus because they lived in the same town and he was introduced to Him by his brother Andrew, who was at first a disciple of John the Baptist before becoming Jesus' disciple. Peter had both high and low points as a disciple.

Among the highs:

- He witnessed miracles performed by Jesus (Matthew 14:22-33).

- He was present at Jesus' transfiguration (Matthew 17:2).

- Peter saw and spoke to Jesus after His resurrection (John 21:15-17).

Some of the lows:

- He was severely reprimanded by Jesus for suggesting that the Lord avoid the cross (Matthew 16:23).

- Peter denied knowing Jesus (three times). This event was recorded by all four gospel writers (John 18:13-27).

3. Peter, a leader in the church

Paul says that along with James and John, Peter was a "pillar" or leader in the early church.

- He was the first to preach the gospel after Jesus' resurrection and ascension (Acts 2:1-42).

- He stood up to Jewish leaders who threatened him because he was preaching about Jesus openly in Jerusalem (Acts 4:1-6).

- He stood up to Jewish Christians who wanted to deny Gentiles entry into the church (Acts 11:1-18).

4. Peter the author

- He was "uneducated" in the sense that he didn't have the kind of training that the Scribes had.

- His writing style was simple but his ideas profound. Some believe Mark's gospel is Peter's account of his experiences with Jesus dictated to Mark.

- He did write two letters (I and II Peter) to the same group around 64-65 AD, near the end of his life (died in Rome crucified upside down in 67 AD fulfilling Jesus' prophecy in John 21:18).

It is interesting that many study the book of Romans or Galatians to learn about the subject of God's grace, and this is fine, since in these two letters the theory and benefits of God's grace are well explained. But it is in Peter's first letter that we see what grace produces in a person's life, a life like Peter's which was a mixture of good and bad, success and failure, your life, my life.

In Peter's letter we learn about God's grace as it affects our everyday lives. Hopefully, by the end of our study we will have a greater understanding of what God's grace means as well as what it does. Before we do that, however, we must first deal with some incorrect ideas that many people have concerning the subject of God's grace.

What Grace is Not

Many people have unbiblical ideas concerning the subject of God's grace. For example:

1. Liberalism

Some think grace means that you can do what you want to do because as a saved person God will not let you be lost. After all, you're under grace! This idea is unbiblical because Paul says in Romans 6:1, "Shall we continue in sin that grace might increase? May it never be." In this passage the Apostle says that grace is not an excuse to continue sinning without guilt or consequences. Those who are under grace are not free to continue to sin because the Bible says, "The wages of sin is death." (Romans 6:23)

2. Permissiveness

There are others who believe that grace means that when it comes to you, God doesn't care about sin. He's blind to your sins because of grace. In other words, grace somehow transforms God into an indulgent grandfather who literally says, "boys will be boys."

But the Bible says, "For we must all appear before the judgment seat of Christ, that each one may be recompensed for his deeds in the body, according to what he has done, whether good or bad," II Corinthians 5:10. Grace does not mean God ignores or indulges our sins, not a single one; on the contrary, the Bible teaches that God will judge us for every single sin.

3. Worldliness

Some people think that grace is a special permission they have from God to remain worldly. By grace they are going to heaven, so in the meantime, they can just be part of this world until it is time to go:

- No effort at holy living
- No effort at spiritual growth
- No effort at building the kingdom

These are the people who clock in at church just enough times to keep their membership on the rolls. The Bible clearly indicates, however, that those who are saved by grace are also transformed by that grace into something different. Paul says that Christians produce spiritual fruit (love, joy, patience, kindness, faithfulness as well as self-control, etc. - Galatians 5:22-23).

Grace doesn't excuse us from living a holy, pure, fruitful and faithful life, it promotes and permits it.

4. Premeditation

The worst misconception about grace is that you can use it to your advantage. In other words, thinking you can sin now and enjoy it because later on God's grace will cover your misdeeds.

Grace is not something we use to enjoy sinfulness. When we do this, we don't realize that the net effect of this type of thinking is that it hardens our consciences to the point where we can't repent (we don't know how to anymore). This is what the Hebrew writer is talking about in Hebrews 6:4-8, "…where we cannot be renewed again to repentance."

Liberalism, permissiveness, worldliness and premeditation are some of the things that are often mistaken for the blessing of God's grace. Let us now turn to Peter's first epistle and see for ourselves how this Apostle explains the true meaning and function of God's grace.

Introduction - I Peter 1

> ^{1} Peter, an apostle of Jesus Christ, To those who reside as aliens, scattered throughout Pontus, Galatia, Cappadocia, Asia, and Bithynia, who are chosen

Peter begins by introducing himself (letters in those days had the writer introduce himself at the beginning, and the greeting at the end). He immediately establishes his credentials and authority as not just any Apostle (messenger) but an Apostle chosen by Christ Himself. The letter is directed to churches scattered throughout Asia Minor (modern day Turkey) and would be passed around among them upon reception.

> ^{2} according to the foreknowledge of God the Father, by the sanctifying work of the Spirit, to obey Jesus Christ and be sprinkled with His blood: May grace and peace be yours in the fullest measure.

He offers a blessing upon them and gives the reason why they should receive it. The blessing is that grace and peace be upon them in full measure.

The reason for them to have access to this is fourfold, and I list these in reverse order for the sake of clarity:

1. Jesus died and shed His blood to wash away their sins.

2. They obeyed the gospel in repentance and baptism to access this blood of Christ.

3. The Holy Spirit has filled them and continued to work in them.

4. God knew from the beginning that all those who would accept Christ would have these blessings.

He prays that the blessings of grace and peace, as a result of their salvation through Christ, known and promised by God, would result in them experiencing the joys produced by these blessings.

In the next verses, he will explain that one of the joys and meanings of this grace he wishes upon them is security or hope.

Grace Means Security - vs. 3-12

In verses 3-5, Peter explains that since salvation and the grace that flows from it comes from God, it is therefore secure.

> ³ Blessed be the God and Father of our Lord Jesus Christ, who according to His great mercy has caused us to be born again to a living hope through the resurrection of Jesus Christ from the dead,

It was God's plan to save us through the death, burial and resurrection of Christ. Salvation and its accompanying grace is not a human invention, it is a Godly thing. It is born of God's plan.

> ⁴ to obtain an inheritance which is imperishable and undefiled and will not fade away, reserved in heaven for you,

Because salvation comes from God, it is a powerful and sure thing. The inheritance he speaks of is the glorified body and eternal life that we, as Christians, experience after we are resurrected from the dead at the end of the world when Jesus returns. This gift, through grace (God's favor), is sure. It will not be destroyed like a material inheritance would. It will be revealed at the resurrection when Jesus comes.

> [6] In this you greatly rejoice, even though now for a little while, if necessary, you have been distressed by various trials, [7] so that the proof of your faith, being more precious than gold which is perishable, even though tested by fire, may be found to result in praise and glory and honor at the revelation of Jesus Christ; [8] and though you have not seen Him, you love Him, and though you do not see Him now, but believe in Him, you greatly rejoice with joy inexpressible and full of glory, [9] obtaining as the outcome of your faith the salvation of your souls.

This sure gift (glorified body, eternal life) is the cause of rejoicing and happy anticipation. However, in the meantime, there may be suffering involved while we wait for it. Remaining faithful while waiting for this gift of grace does several things:

1. Confirms that our faith is genuine. If a person endures while the going is rough, it demonstrates that his faith is real, not just talk. (James 3:18)

2. It honors Jesus Christ. Suffering in patience is a demonstration of love and loyalty to the Lord, and genuinely honors Him. (Romans 12:1)

3. It generates joy and love within. Jesus said, "Blessed (happy) are those who have been persecuted for the sake of righteousness, for theirs is the kingdom of heaven." (Matthew 5:10) Suffering righteously for the

Lord produces happiness and is a natural reaction for the spiritual person.

4. It guarantees salvation. A proven faith results in a secure hope of salvation which produces peace and joy in one's heart. (James 1:3-4)

And so, Peter tells his readers that grace means feeling sure about salvation even though there are times when one's faith is tested. Continuing in faith will only strengthen that hope and increase the joy that one feels.

> [10] As to this salvation, the prophets who prophesied of the grace that would come to you made careful searches and inquiries, [11] seeking to know what person or time the Spirit of Christ within them was indicating as He predicted the sufferings of Christ and the glories to follow. [12] It was revealed to them that they were not serving themselves, but you, in these things which now have been announced to you through those who preached the gospel to you by the Holy Spirit sent from heaven—things into which angels long to look.

In the last three verses of this section, Peter compares his readers to two other groups in order to show how secure they are in Christ.

- The prophets, who spoke from God, did miracles, counseled kings and saved the nation.

- Angels, who are mighty beings, stand before the throne of God.

Peter states, however, that neither of these groups received the revelation about God's gracious plan to save men through faith in Jesus Christ, and give them glorious bodies to live forever with Christ in heaven. Even though they were mighty servants who searched for the answers, all they knew was that God's plan was to serve people in the future. We are those people and this is how we are in the "Book of Life."

God's grace is no afterthought. It was planned for and passed on carefully throughout the ages until the right moment arrived for it to be revealed to the world so all could receive its blessings.

Summary

Peter begins his epistle by explaining that the grace of God is a sure thing. When we think of His grace (His favor towards us) we can feel secure. Peter explains why this is so:

1. It comes from God. When a promise of blessing comes directly from God, we can be sure that we will receive it.

2. It grows stronger with adversity. The promise of grace itself cannot be diminished by trials. The harder one struggles to remain faithful, the more His grace produces in terms of joy, hope and security.

3. It has lasted throughout the ages. Long ago angels and prophets handled it and passed it down. We receive His grace today as it forgives us and grants us eternal life. The promise and its effect on us is as fresh and motivating as it was 4000 years ago when God announced it to Abraham.

Grace means security. Security in God's desire and ability to fulfill His promises to bless us now and save us forever.

We sometimes doubt or are afraid of the past or perhaps an uncertain future, but God's grace has wiped away the past with Jesus' blood and guaranteed the future with His resurrection. The knowledge of this is how one is able to live in the "now."

In the chapters to come, we will continue with other meanings of grace, but for now we will remain with security. If you have received the grace of God through Christ, you can be sure of your eternal salvation. For this reason, we should not be afraid to go through whatever trials are before us in order to remain faithful. Jesus never said it would be easy, but His promise of grace assures us that whatever we suffer to remain faithful will be worth it when He comes.

CHAPTER 2
The Meaning of Grace:
SOBRIETY

I Peter 1:13-2:10

We are studying both the life and the first epistle of Peter the Apostle in order to gain a better understanding of the biblical concept of grace. Our basic idea of grace is that it is either:

- A character trait of God referring to His kindness, His mercy, His generosity (a gracious God, the God of grace).

- What God gives (unmerited favor; a gift that we don't deserve).

The character of God and His blessings on us also create something within us as we come in contact with Him and the blessings He generously gives. Grace takes on new meanings for those exposed to it:

- For Peter it meant transition from fisherman to Apostle to church leader and inspired martyr.

- For those of us who come to know God and His salvation through Peter's preaching, grace has come to mean several things.

In our last chapter, we said that grace also meant security. When we think and experience God's grace, we also experience the secure knowledge that the blessings He gives actually:

1. Come from the only divine Lord
2. Grow stronger with adversity
3. Will last forever

To know the grace of God, is to know what security really means and feels like. We can look for security and safety in all kinds of people, things and institutions in this world, but Peter tells us that the only way to feel true security is to experience the grace of God.

In the next section of his epistle, Peter explains that grace also means Sobriety.

As I mentioned in the previous chapter, some people think that grace means that God allows a person to simply go ahead and live his life in the way he has always lived it, except now because of this grace thing, he is going to heaven. But to know God's grace means that you not only experience security for the first time, you also experience sobriety for the first time. While we are lost sinners, we are under the influence of sin, the world and Satan himself. This influence makes us think, say and do all kinds of things. Paul names some of them in Galatians 5:19-21:

> [19] Now the deeds of the flesh are evident, which are: immorality, impurity, sensuality, [20] idolatry, sorcery, enmities, strife, jealousy, outbursts of anger, disputes, dissensions, factions, [21] envying,

> drunkenness, carousing, and things like these, of which I forewarn you, just as I have forewarned you, that those who practice such things will not inherit the kingdom of God.

Peter says that when we are saved by Jesus Christ we come under the influence of grace, and grace produces sobriety (we're not drunk with sin anymore). This sobriety manifests itself in four different ways:

1. It Manifests Itself in Holiness — 1:13-16

> [13] Therefore, prepare your minds for action, keep sober in spirit, fix your hope completely on the grace to be brought to you at the revelation of Jesus Christ.

Soberness requires one to be focused on what is important, and ready to challenge anything that threatens what is important. In our case what is important is the second coming of Christ and our resurrection at that time. Nothing should distract us from this goal.

> [14] As obedient children, do not be conformed to the former lusts which were yours in your ignorance, [15] but like the Holy One who called you, be holy yourselves also in all your behavior; [16] because it is written, "You shall be holy, for I am holy."

Grace has put us into the position of receiving eternal life and the blessings of heaven. In order to receive these, we must not go back to being under the influence of sin but rather let ourselves be influenced by grace, and this grace will lead us to holy behavior. Holy behavior is behavior that reflects the character of God and Christ Jesus. The word "holy" means separate.

The priests were holy because through their selection, ceremonial clothing and work they separated themselves from the dress, work and calling of ordinary people. A place or a thing became holy because it was set aside for a special religious purpose.

Peter says that we become holy by separating ourselves from the things we used to do and say when we were under the influence of sin.

Grace leads to sobriety and sobriety enables us to understand and obey God's commands. This obedience separates us from the normal activity in the world. This separation from sinful and worldly habits is what makes us holy.

2. Sobriety Manifests Itself in Fear — 1:17-21

One of the more sobering experiences of being saved is realizing that if there is a heaven, then there is also a hell.

> The fool has said in his heart, "There is no God." They are corrupt, they have committed abominable deeds; There is no one who does good.
> - Psalm 14:1

Many go through life daring death, reviling angels and God, not having a clue that God will require their souls one day.

Grace brings us to the understanding of how close we came to being lost forever.

> [17] If you address as Father the One who impartially judges according to each one's work, conduct yourselves in fear during the time of your stay on earth; [18] knowing that you were not redeemed with perishable things like silver or gold from your futile way of life inherited from your forefathers, [19] but with precious blood, as of a lamb unblemished and spotless, the blood of Christ. [20] For He was foreknown before the foundation of the world, but has appeared in these last times for the sake of you [21] who through Him are believers in God, who raised Him from the dead and gave Him glory, so that your faith and hope are in God.

Peter says that if you really do believe:

- That God is the Almighty Judge
- That He sacrificed His only Son for you
- That this was God's plan from the beginning (that you be saved and go to heaven)

If you know and believe these things, then you should behave yourself and walk in fear and respect of the One who has the power of life and death over you. Grace means that God has exercised His power to save you rather than punish you, but this realization should produce a healthy respect. Everyone will be judged:

- Some will be judged guilty and punished.
- Some will be judged faithful and spared.

We should live soberly and respectfully knowing that all (including us) will receive that judgment.

… Grace leads to sobriety and manifests itself in holiness, fear…

3. Sobriety Manifests Itself in Love — 1:22-25

Grace produces new behavior. There is the new behavior seen as things we don't do anymore (immorality, hatred, carousing, etc.) and, as Peter explains, there are now things that we do which were not evident before.

> [22] Since you have in obedience to the truth purified your souls for a sincere love of the brethren, fervently love one another from the heart, [23] for you have been born again not of seed which is perishable but imperishable, that is, through the living and enduring word of God. [24] For,
> "All flesh is like grass,
> And all its glory like the flower of grass.
> The grass withers,
> And the flower falls off,
> [25] But the word of the Lord endures forever."
> And this is the word which was preached to you.

Here he explains that the very special love that Christians have for one another produced by the Word of God in their hearts is like a seed bearing rich fruit. In the world, we loved ourselves and sin and the things of this world, but under the sobriety produced by the influence of grace, God through His holy Word is producing a special kind of love that only Christians share. We are no longer seduced by the love of the flesh and the vanity of life, but now quite deliberately choose to love our brethren with a forgiving, sacrificial love that reflects the love that Christ showed for us on the cross.

The Word of God produces agape love which is love that is unselfish, asexual and uncompromising. It produces a kind of love that we have never experienced before. Grace equals sobriety, and sobriety leads us to holiness, respect and love.

4. Sobriety Manifests Itself in Growth — 2:1-10

The spiritual sobriety generated by God's grace provides the right environment and motivation for personal growth. The purpose of sobriety is to allow us the state of mind and spirit that can perceive and experience why we were saved in the first place.

> [1] Therefore, putting aside all malice and all deceit and hypocrisy and envy and all slander, [2] like newborn babies, long for the pure milk of the word, so that by it you may grow in respect to salvation, [3] if you have tasted the kindness of the Lord.
>
> [4] And coming to Him as to a living stone which has been rejected by men, but is choice and precious in the sight of God, [5] you also, as living stones, are being built up as a spiritual house for a holy priesthood, to offer up spiritual sacrifices acceptable to God through Jesus Christ.

Peter says that once you begin to live in holiness, respect for God and love, you begin to fulfill the original purpose of God's grace and that is to build you into the church. We often say, "the church is not the building, the people are the church." Peter goes one step beyond this saying, "not only are the people the church, but the purpose of these people in life is to make pleasing offerings to God." Paul explains in Romans 12:1-2 and Ephesians 5:15-20 that these sacrifices consist of two things:

1. A holy style of living filled with service.
2. A joyful heart full of spiritual praise.

He then goes another step by describing the true identity of these people who are the church.

> ⁶ For this is contained in Scripture:
> "Behold, I lay in Zion a choice stone, a precious corner stone,
> And he who believes in Him will not be disappointed."
>
> ⁷ This precious value, then, is for you who believe; but for those who disbelieve,
> "The stone which the builders rejected,
> This became the very corner stone,"
> ⁸ and,
> "A stone of stumbling and a rock of offense";
> for they stumble because they are disobedient to the word, and to this doom they were also appointed.
>
> ⁹ But you are a chosen race, a royal priesthood, a holy nation, a people for God's own possession, so that you may proclaim the excellencies of Him who has called you out of darkness into His marvelous light; ¹⁰ for you once were not a people, but now you are the people of God; you had not received mercy, but now you have received mercy.

The priests and Levites in the Old Testament were not allowed strong drink while they served at the temple. They had to remain sober in order to carry out their tasks. The point that Peter is making is that grace leads us to the spiritual sobriety we need to function in our new roles as: the chosen race and Royal priests.

An interesting note is that in Old Testament times the kings could not offer sacrifice and the priests couldn't be kings. Only Melchizedek in the Old Testament and Christ in the New Testament were both kings and priests. Now Christians are added to that group: Holy nation.

These were titles enjoyed by the Jews in one way or another for a time, but now through the grace of Christ, they have been conferred on those who believe and follow Jesus. Like any other role or position, a person has to "grow into" the situation. Peter says that through the sobering effect of grace, we are prepared to enter into and function in our new roles as God's chosen, holy nation of royal priests, building His kingdom through holy living, praise and Christian witness.

Summary

The grace of God is at work before, during and after our salvation:

- **Before**: God from the beginning of time has been planning and working towards the salvation of sinners.

- **During**: When we believe, confess, repent and are baptized, the grace of God, through the cross of Christ, washes away our sins and fills us with His Holy Spirit.

- **After**: Following the moment of our salvation, the grace of God continues to be effective in our lives.

It provides a feeling and knowledge of security as well as reassurance that God will fulfill His promises to us. It releases us from the influence of sin and leads us to spiritual sobriety which manifests itself in:

- A holy living style
- A new fear or respect for God
- A different kind of love for those who believe (Christian love)
- Development as royal priests offering sacrifices of service, praise and witness

CHAPTER 3
The Meaning of Grace:
SUBMISSION

I Peter 2:1-3:7

Submission is not a socially or culturally popular idea in the time we live in. For example, the USA was established through revolution and its citizens pride themselves on having the freedom to say or do anything, anytime and anywhere. Much of our entertainment, especially comedy, is based on the ridicule of our leaders. Most of our heroes are men and women who defy authority and get away with it.

It is difficult to cultivate a true Christian culture of submission in this type of environment. In his first epistle, Peter the Apostle says that the experience of God's grace will eventually create a person who:

- Feels secure in salvation
- Changes his lifestyle to include:
  - Holy living habits
  - Greater respect for God
  - New way of loving
  - Different self-image

The Christian is no longer a sinner, a worldly person, a rebel, but now has become a royal priest, a chosen person belonging to a holy nation. In addition to these Peter shows that God's grace enables a person to understand and accept that an important part of a Christian's character is the ability to submit.

Peter shows that grace in one's life means that a person is able to submit to all the forms of authority that God has established so that order can be maintained in the world, in the family and in the kingdom.

Rebellion vs. Submission

The root of many problems is rebellion. Before Adam sinned, there was rebellion in the heavens. The Bible doesn't give many details, but Jude tells us in verse 6 that the angels rebelled in refusing to keep the positions that God assigned to them and were cast down by God. It was one of those rebellious angels, Lucifer, who in the guise of a serpent, tempted Eve who caused the fall of mankind. The dictionary defines rebellion as:

1. The refusal to accept authority
2. To defy control by another
3. To oppose authority, government, law

Aside from the commands in the Bible that we obey God's laws, we are also bound to obey the law and the government of the land. Peter refers to the spirit of rebellion that exists in sinful people who resist every kind of authority and secretly desire to do only what *they* want to do. He explains that God's grace, acting in peoples' lives, changes their basic aversion to any kind of authority into one of submission to all forms of legitimate authority.

Rebellion means to refuse, defy and oppose all forms of authority. Submission means a new attitude towards authority.

Submit — to submit is a military term which means to "place oneself under." For example, a military person sees a group of military people with varying ranks and places himself under the ones that outrank him.

Submission includes two actions:

1. **Recognition** - the recognition of one's position, whether it is an assigned one or a position based on age, skill, etc. Submission requires that we see the "big picture" and recognize where we stand in relation to everyone else.

2. **Willingness** - Biblical submission is not defeat, it is an act of the will in accepting a role, position or task. Submission is not slavery because slaves have no choice; submission is a positive response to accept our rightful place whether that place is first or last.

We live in an ordered universe, an order created by God to provide for the greatest human fulfillment and joy. The problems began when the angels refused to keep their positions in this order (they either wanted to be on God's throne or they refused to serve man) and instead, tried to destroy man.

Once created, humans wanted to leave their positions (they wanted to be in God's position to know good and evil). The result was spiritual rebellion, sin and destruction. After this initial rebellion God established a temporary order that had three layers: government, society and family. These were established to guarantee some form of harmony in this sinful world until Jesus would return and a new order would be established never to be challenged again.

People continue to rebel against this temporary order in many ways, causing all kinds of problems. Peter says that when a person experiences God's saving grace, that grace neutralizes that rebellious spirit and that person is able to:

1. Recognize the big picture and see his/her place in God's plan.

2. Willingly take their place, whatever that is, in order to serve and glorify God. Rebellion does not glorify God, but accepting one's place willingly and profitably, this glorifies God and contributes to peace on earth and the growth of the kingdom.

In chapters 2 and 3, Peter reviews how grace means submission in these three areas.

1. Grace Enables Submission to Government — 2:11-17

> [11] Beloved, I urge you as aliens and strangers to abstain from fleshly lusts which wage war against the soul. [12] Keep your behavior excellent among the Gentiles, so that in the thing in which they slander you as evildoers, they may because of your good deeds, as they observe them, glorify God in the day of visitation.

As Christians, they lived in the same environment as the pagans did and therefore were subject to the same temptations and pressures. Peter tells them that as Christians they are to act in a manner befitting their calling, and in so doing win the respect of the non-believers. These Christians had left paganism and were being criticized by their pagan friends and relatives for leaving their old religions. Peter says that their good conduct may work in such a way as to win these people over to the very religion they criticized and end up glorifying God themselves.

It was especially important to have good conduct because in those days the criticism and some persecution were also coming from the government. God authorizes the idea of human government but does not specify or bless a particular form (kings, governors, presidents, chiefs). Peter shows them that part of this acceptable behavior includes respect and obedience for the "form" of government that existed at that time.

> [13] Submit yourselves for the Lord's sake to every human institution, whether to a king as the one in authority, [14] or to governors as sent by him for the punishment of evildoers and the praise of those who do right. [15] For such is the will of God that by doing right you may silence the ignorance of foolish men. [16] Act as free men, and do not use your freedom as a covering for evil, but use it as bondslaves of God. [17] Honor all people, love the brotherhood, fear God, honor the king.

How and why are Christians to submit to civil authority?

- They submit to civil authority because it has been established by God in order to preserve order in society. This is so, regardless of the form or style it takes.

- Peter says to do so will remove any chance for non-believers to lend criticism at Christians.

- He also says that the secret of living under any kind of human authority (whether it is democratic like the USA or despotic like Iran) is to realize three things:

    1. We are free from God's condemnation and thus are truly free.

    2. Our purpose is to establish the kingdom of heaven on earth, not any human kingdom on earth. Let the unbelievers worry about this.

    3. We are slaves of God and so no one can truly enslave us.

Grace means that we submit to our human rulers because in doing so we can carry out our true purpose in life, and that is to serve our heavenly ruler. Grace means submission to government.

2. Grace Enables Submission to Our Masters — 2:18-25

In that day, slavery was the common social connection between employer and employee. Today, in most of the world, slavery does not exist anymore, but Peter's teaching here applies to every relationship where one is in charge and one must report.

> [18] Servants, be submissive to your masters with all respect, not only to those who are good and gentle, but also to those who are unreasonable.

Peter says that what counts as a Christian is your attitude, not the attitude of your boss. To be obedient and compliant to our bosses, managers, etc., is our choice, made easier or harder by them, but always remains our choice.

> [19] For this finds favor, if for the sake of conscience toward God a person bears up under sorrows when suffering unjustly. [20] For what credit is there if, when you sin and are harshly treated, you endure it with patience? But if when you do what is right and suffer for it you patiently endure it, this finds favor with God.

The purpose for *our* attitude is our faith and desire to please God. If we endure injustice patiently, this pleases God. If we suffer because of our own rebellion, we get what we deserve.

The objective in employee/employer relationships is not to win points, rights, concessions, but to please God and win our boss' respect and soul.

> [21] For you have been called for this purpose, since Christ also suffered for you, leaving you an example for you to follow in His steps, [22] who committed no sin, nor was any deceit found in His mouth; [23] and while being reviled, He did not revile in return; while suffering, He uttered no threats, but kept entrusting Himself to Him who judges righteously; [24] and He Himself bore our sins in His body on the cross, so that we might die to sin and live to righteousness; for by His wounds you were healed. [25] For you were continually straying like sheep, but now you have returned to the Shepherd and Guardian of your souls.

Peter says that the purpose we have been called (to become disciples of Christ) is to continue portraying His examples of:

- Pure living (no sin)
- Patience in suffering (did not revile His attackers)
- Soul winning (by His example we were saved)

Christ could have beaten both the Jews and Romans with His army of angels, but instead, through His patience and submission to the Father, He won some of their souls. There is a big difference between winning the game or the war, and winning a soul.

An important thing to remember during the day-to-day grind of dealing with our superiors in school, work, etc., is that the objective is not to win over them, but to win them over, and the first step towards this is submission to government and those who have authority over us.

3. Grace Means Submission in the Family — 3:1-7

The most intimate relationship, however, is the family, and Peter shows how the spirit of submission works to order this area as well.

> [1] In the same way, you wives, be submissive to your own husbands so that even if any of them are disobedient to the word, they may be won without a word by the behavior of their wives,

Peter speaks to those who are married to pagans because it seems that there may have been a question as to the Christian woman's role in such a situation. The submission of a wife to her husband was a clearly established idea in

Jewish culture, but Paul, and now Peter, confirm that this is God's purpose for all married relationships in order to maintain order and peace. The extra dimension here is that this type of behavior is the only way a Christian woman will achieve her ultimate goal, the salvation of her mate.

> [2] as they observe your chaste and respectful behavior. [3] Your adornment must not be merely external—braiding the hair, and wearing gold jewelry, or putting on dresses; [4] but let it be the hidden person of the heart, with the imperishable quality of a gentle and quiet spirit, which is precious in the sight of God. [5] For in this way in former times the holy women also, who hoped in God, used to adorn themselves, being submissive to their own husbands; [6] just as Sarah obeyed Abraham, calling him lord, and you have become her children if you do what is right without being frightened by any fear.

Here, Peter details the character of a submissive wife:

1. She is not spiritually bossy (verse 1). "Without a word" means without showing off her spiritual knowledge or pointing out her husband's spiritual failures.

2. Pure and respectful (verse 2). Sexually pure as a good witness. Respectful in the sense that the submission is sincere and not merely lip service.

3. Confidence — submission doesn't mean slavery. A Christian woman has character, strength and peace which are her inner beauty. These are the things she concentrates on rather than outward beauty. These are the things that her husband will notice and continue to cherish long after the outward beauty will fade.

Sarah was such a woman and it was her strength and peace that enabled her to submit to Abraham, not fear.

> [7] You husbands in the same way, live with your wives in an understanding way, as with someone weaker, since she is a woman; and show her honor as a fellow heir of the grace of life, so that your prayers will not be hindered.

Now Peter speaks to Christian husbands on the flip side of this issue. Pagan husbands will act as they will with only the Christian attitude of their wives to save them.

Christian husbands, however, have the responsibility to *know* (understand) their wives and the special needs that they have because they are women and mothers, and asked by God to submit to their husbands. For husbands not to carefully provide that understanding and care is to hinder their own spiritual lives. The best compliment from a wife to her husband is when she is able to say to him, "You know me so well."

Submission doesn't mean slavery and Peter reminds men of the equal value and rewards that God sees women as having. Grace enables a woman to willfully accept a role she would normally reject or overthrow with her intelligence and guile; the same grace enables a man to keep in check his natural tendency to dominate by force one who is weaker.

Submission is God's way of guaranteeing balance and peace in the family until Jesus returns when there will only be one family.

Summary

Peter tracks the various effects on a person's life as God's grace leads him to experience a spirit of submission.

A change that includes a willingness to accept and submit to authority where it has been established by God: in society, in one's career, as well as in the home.

This new attitude produces a good witness for Christ wherever we are, and guarantees peace and harmony which are pleasing to God.

Of course, our very first act of submission that God's grace calls us to perform leads to our greatest eternal blessing. God calls on everyone to accept Jesus Christ as His only divine Son and submit to Him by confessing His name, repenting of sin and being baptized (Acts 2:36-38).

CHAPTER 4
The Meaning of Grace:
SUFFERING

I Peter 3:8-4:19

We are studying the concept of grace as Peter explains it in his first epistle. When he talks about grace, he is referring to two things:

1. God's work throughout the ages to save man's soul through Jesus Christ, the preaching of His gospel and the work of His church.

2. The effect that this salvation has had on those who have been saved.

This epistle concentrates more on the effects of salvation because the gospels have already described God's work through Christ to save man. So far in our study Peter says that the effect of grace (salvation of one's soul) is seen in several ways:

1. **Security** — People are no longer afraid of death and condemnation or an angry God.

2. **Sobriety** (not under the influence of sin) — More holy living, respect for God, Christian love and spiritual mindedness.

3. **Submission** — Knowing one's place in God's plan and not rebelling against it.

In the following section, Peter will add a fourth effect of grace on one's individual life: suffering. Before developing this idea however, he takes a pause and describes how grace affects Christians as a group.

Grace and the Church — I Peter 3:8-12

So far Peter has been explaining how grace affects the individual. What should a person who is not a Christian see when they look at a person who has experienced grace? Peter explains that they should see signs of a person who feels secure, lives a sober life and is in submission to God and those over him.

In addition to this, Peter says that grace also affects these people as a group (we call the church) because this group will interact with itself, the government, society and other families in a much different way than those groups who have not been touched by the grace of God.

Peter explains that difference in the next few verses:

> ⁸ To sum up, all of you be harmonious, sympathetic, brotherly, kindhearted, and humble in spirit;

The group that has been touched by grace has certain noticeable features:

- **Harmony** — Same minded, of one mind, not in division or conflict

- **Sympathy** — Sharing the feelings of others

- **Brotherly** — Kind, brotherly kindness

- **Kindhearted** — Compassionate (especially for those outside)

- **Humble in spirit** — Not proud or self-centered

> [9] not returning evil for evil or insult for insult, but giving a blessing instead; for you were called for the very purpose that you might inherit a blessing.

The true spirit of Christ lives among them in that they turn the other cheek when wronged and seek peace rather than winning at all cost. Peter says that the motivation for offering a blessing is that Christians are the only ones that have blessings to look forward to, so they, as a group, can offer them now.

> [10] For,
> "The one who desires life, to love and see good days,
> Must keep his tongue from evil and his lips from speaking deceit.
> [11] "He must turn away from evil and do good;
> He must seek peace and pursue it.
> [12] "For the eyes of the Lord are toward the righteous,
> And His ears attend to their prayer,
> But the face of the Lord is against those who do evil."

This is a quote from Psalm 34 and Peter uses it to remind them of two things:

1. Much of the behavior he mentions before is possible if one is able to control and use his tongue properly and avoid evil practice. Evil speech leads to evil deeds, and evil deeds destroy peace and harmony. This is not a mark of grace.

2. God blesses the group that acts in harmony, sympathy, brotherly love, etc., but he punishes and works against those who speak evil and do evil.

He uses this last idea (God blessing the good and punishing the evil) to open up his fourth meaning regarding grace, that grace may mean suffering.

In the Sermon on the Mount, Jesus says that His disciples are blessed (happy) if they suffer on His account or because they are pursuing what is right (Matthew 5:10-12). Peter echoes this idea now when he refers to the suffering experienced by those who have received grace. Grace doesn't necessarily cause suffering, but those who experience grace often experience suffering because of their faith, and Peter refers to this kind of suffering (persecution) now.

He says that at times grace does mean that Christians have to suffer and, when they do suffer persecution, they should remember several things about this experience:

1. Don't be Afraid

> [13] Who is there to harm you if you prove zealous for what is good? [14] But even if you should suffer for the sake of righteousness, you are blessed. And do not fear their intimidation, and do not be troubled,

The harm is not physical harm but spiritual harm. The enemies of right can only kill the body but cannot take away a believer's "life." Grace gives us the power to not be afraid of wrong and of those who oppose God.

2. Don't be Quiet

> [15] but sanctify Christ as Lord in your hearts, always being ready to make a defense to everyone who asks you to give an account for the hope that is in you, yet with gentleness and reverence; [16] and keep a good conscience so that in the thing in which you are slandered, those who revile your good behavior in Christ will be put to shame.

Grace gives one the courage to withstand and oppose what is wrong by using the gospel of Christ. Peter explains that our response should be given in humility and respect. Christians don't destroy abortion clinics, don't attack homosexuals, don't take up arms against the government simply because they don't agree with certain policies or moral standards.

Grace gives the follower of Christ confidence to respond to ignorance and immorality with the truth and power of the gospel preached in love and with respect.

Peter mentions that our response should not only be in words, but in deeds that reflect our words. This type of confidence, this type of witness, he says, will win the respect of enemies and prove that their reasons for attacking us in the first place are groundless.

3. Don't Suffer for the Wrong Reason

> ¹⁷ For it is better, if God should will it so, that you suffer for doing what is right rather than for doing what is wrong.

If a person suffers for wrong-doing, cowardice or rebellion, there is no glory in this. But if a person does right and suffers for it, the experience may be unpleasant, but it is pleasing to God. In the next section he explains why this is so. It was this kind of suffering that Christ experienced which led to the salvation of our souls.

> ¹⁸ For Christ also died for sins once for all, the just for the unjust, so that He might bring us to God, having been put to death in the flesh, but made alive in the spirit;

In other words, suffering for right does have positive effects.

In verses 19-22, he gives the example that Christ's suffering, even though it led to death, provided positive results for those who believe.

> ¹⁹ in which also He went and made proclamation to the spirits now in prison, ²⁰ who once were disobedient, when the patience of God kept waiting in the days of Noah, during the construction of the ark, in which a few, that is, eight persons, were brought safely through the water.

1. His suffering caused death, but His death provided Him with the opportunity to show Himself to the

unbelievers who had made believers suffer on His account in the past.

2. Peter chooses Noah as a good example of one who suffered for righteousness. He explains that Noah is now justified as Christ proclaims the gospel to unbelieving spirits in hell, not to save them, but to show them that they were wrong and that Noah and other righteous men and women who suffered righteously were right all along.

In other words, we "go" into all the world to preach the gospel, but Jesus can and has gone everywhere, even into the spiritual dimension (hell) to proclaim the gospel. Therefore, those who suffer for Christ can now take courage because one day His return appearance will silence the modern day mockers and doubters, and confirm that we were right to believe and suffer for Him.

Another positive benefit of Christ's suffering…

> [21] Corresponding to that, baptism now saves you—not the removal of dirt from the flesh, but an appeal to God for a good conscience—through the resurrection of Jesus Christ, [22] who is at the right hand of God, having gone into heaven, after angels and authorities and powers had been subjected to Him.

His suffering also sets the stage for His resurrection, ascension and exaltation to God's throne of grace. If He had refused the suffering, He could not have sat at the throne of God and offered us the grace of forgiveness received at baptism.

Peter uses this opportunity to show that their baptism was not a mere ceremony or symbol, but embodied the actual way that they received the forgiveness from sin that was obtained through Christ's sufferings.

Let us not forget our main idea here, that we should be prepared to suffer for Christ because this is pleasing to God and produces spiritual benefits. Jesus is an example of this:

- His suffering proved to all unbelievers (even in the spiritual dimension) that they were wrong and the believers were right.

- His suffering purchased the forgiveness for our sins received through faith, expressed in the waters of baptism.

Suffering is never pleasant, but if we share in the sufferings of Christ, we will also share in His glorious resurrection, glorification and exaltation.

4. Don't be Seduced

> [1] Therefore, since Christ has suffered in the flesh, arm yourselves also with the same purpose, because he who has suffered in the flesh has ceased from sin, [2] so as to live the rest of the time in the flesh no longer for the lusts of men, but for the will of God. [3] For the time already past is sufficient for you to have carried out the desire of the Gentiles, having pursued a course of sensuality, lusts, drunkenness, carousing, drinking parties and abominable idolatries. [4] In all this, they are surprised that you do not run with them into the same excesses of dissipation, and they malign you; [5] but they will give account to Him who is ready to judge the living and the dead. [6] For the gospel has for this purpose been preached even to those who are dead, that though they are judged in the flesh as men, they

> may live in the spirit according to the will of God.

When people have to suffer because of their faith, it is easy for them to quit following Jesus, and having nowhere else to go, they return to their former sinful lifestyle. Peter reminds them that grace has taken them out of the world and saved them from the judgment to come.

We shouldn't be fooled, both the promise of salvation for the faithful and condemnation of the unfaithful are equally true.

5. Don't Give Up

> [7] The end of all things is near; therefore, be of sound judgment and sober spirit for the purpose of prayer. [8] Above all, keep fervent in your love for one another, because love covers a multitude of sins. [9] Be hospitable to one another without complaint. [10] As each one has received a special gift, employ it in serving one another as good stewards of the manifold grace of God. [11] Whoever speaks, is to do so as one who is speaking the utterances of God; whoever serves is to do so as one who is serving by the strength which God supplies; so that in all things God may be glorified through Jesus Christ, to whom belongs the glory and dominion forever and ever. Amen.

Suffering, obstacles of faith, the sinfulness and disbelief of others are all discouraging. Peter exhorts his readers, then and now, to not give up living as Christians each day. In this section he mentions several things that can be maintained despite suffering:

- Remain sober-minded, don't get panicky or depressed.
- Remain fervent in prayer.
- Remain loving and hospitable.
- Remain helpful, using your talents to serve and build up one another.

Hard times and persecution do not have to destroy how we treat each other in the church, especially persecution that is caused by one's faith. On the contrary, suffering for Christ usually brings out these things in abundance and helps the church to grow.

6. Don't be Surprised

> [12] Beloved, do not be surprised at the fiery ordeal among you, which comes upon you for your testing, as though some strange thing were happening to you; [13] but to the degree that you share the sufferings of Christ, keep on rejoicing, so that also at the revelation of His glory you may rejoice with exultation. [14] If you are reviled for the name of Christ, you are blessed, because the Spirit of glory and of God rests on you. [15] Make sure that none of you suffers as a murderer, or thief, or evildoer, or a troublesome meddler; [16] but if anyone suffers as a Christian, he is not to be ashamed, but is to glorify God in this name. [17] For it is time for judgment to begin with the household of God; and if it begins with us first, what will be the outcome for those who do not obey the gospel of God? [18] And if it is with difficulty that the righteous is saved, what will become of the godless man and the sinner? [19] Therefore, those also who suffer according to the will of God shall entrust their souls to a faithful

> Creator in doing what is right.

Peter says that if the Lord of the church, who was perfect and sinless, was cursed and killed, why should we be surprised when His followers are persecuted? He teaches us that God permits our suffering for His own purposes and our good:

- Suffering provides an opportunity to test or examine our faith and maturity to see what needs strengthening. When there is no testing it is difficult to know what needs fixing or improvement.

- Suffering provides an opportunity to more fully reveal Christ to those who do not believe.

- Suffering for Christ is a privilege and a proof of God's presence in the believer's life. After all, they don't persecute unbelievers for their disbelief.

Peter finishes this section with a reminder that he is talking about suffering for Christ, not suffering for sin. Suffering for Christ is a necessary part of a Christian's life and we shouldn't be surprised when it happens. We should rejoice and glorify God for the privilege since we understand the purpose, nature and blessing of it. Pity those who do not know God's grace and have disobeyed the gospel. Imagine their suffering!

In the end, the way to cope with suffering is to trust God completely for two reasons:

1. He is faithful. He will fulfill His promises to not burden us with more than we can carry, and to resurrect us in the end.
2. He is righteous. No matter what, He will always do what is right.

Summary

Peter explains that grace leads us to suffering at times, and when it does we need to remember several things:

1. Don't be afraid, God is our shield.
2. Don't be quiet, the gospel is our voice.
3. Don't suffer for wrong, happy are those who suffer for Christ's sake.
4. Don't be seduced, God will punish sinners.
5. Don't give up, stay busy in doing good.
6. Don't be surprised, suffering is a normal part of the Christian's life.

To these I add a seventh idea:

7. Don't Procrastinate

If you are suffering guilt and trouble because of your sins, don't hesitate to receive a clean conscience by calling on the name of Jesus (I Peter 3:21) in baptism.

If you've been afraid or quiet, seduced by the world or given up faithful Christian living because of sin or discouragement, make sure you are restored through the prayers of the church.

CHAPTER 5
The Meaning of Grace:
SERVICE

I Peter 5:1-14

Peter understood so well the idea of grace having witnessed the grace of God in both of its contexts:

1. The grace of God seen in the person of Jesus Christ. The gracious way that God had formed the Jewish nation, in order to bring Jesus onto the earth. The love He displayed in allowing Jesus to die for our sins and then raised Him from the dead to show that He was God and had the authority to forgive sins and save man from eternal destruction.

Peter was our eye witness to all of these events that demonstrated God's grace in saving mankind.

2. Peter also understood the idea of grace from a personal perspective as he experienced the changes that God's grace

worked in himself and others who believed in Jesus. His first epistle is a description and explanation of what grace means to one who has been touched by it:

- Grace means a sense of security from the fear of condemnation.

- Grace means a spiritually sober lifestyle no longer addicted to sin and the world.

- Grace means a heartfelt submission to God's will in every area of life and the peace that comes with this.

- Grace means living in harmony with others who have experienced God's love and salvation.

- Grace means suffering at times because those who are saved from the world are often no longer welcomed in it.

In this chapter we will look at the final meaning that Peter ascribes to grace, the last thing he says that grace does to our character when it touches us.

There is an old saying that goes, "We have been saved to serve." God extends His grace to us so that we will become a channel through which His grace can reach others. Our faith and salvation find meaning and satisfaction as we begin to serve God in the work of seeking and saving others.

Peter uses elders as the ultimate example of God's grace at work in the church. A person could not aspire to a more meaningful or gracious role in God's kingdom than to serve His church as an elder.

Peter doesn't describe the work of an elder because he assumes everyone knows that an elder's role is one of complete service. Paul explains in his letters to Timothy and Titus, not only the elder's character, but the work that he has been chosen to do. This includes teaching, offering hospitality, encouraging the brethren and defending the church against false teachers and their doctrines.

Peter reminds them that an important part of an elder's responsibility is to lead, and he uses this opportunity to teach them not only that grace produces leaders who serve, but leaders who serve in a particular way. There may have been some confusion as to the authority and role of the elders among those to whom he is writing, so Peter explains that grace produces leaders who serve in the "Spirit of Christ."

> [1] Therefore, I exhort the elders among you, as your fellow elder and witness of the sufferings of Christ, and a partaker also of the glory that is to be revealed,

The Apostle offers this exhortation (a word of encouragement, motivation) to specific people: elders. In the New Testament, there were three words that referred to the leaders in the church. All pointed to the same person but described him in a different way.

1. **Shepherd (pastor):** referred to the way a man carried out his leadership role. The imagery of the caring, protective, nurturing shepherd was used to describe the men who were to lead the church by shepherding them and doing this by caring, nurturing and protecting the members of the congregation. We get the word pastor from this word and idea.

2. **Bishop/overseer:** these were terms that stressed the authority given by God to these men (if they qualified). Sometimes they were used to describe the leader or the shepherd who was leading the church. They referred to those who were responsible for the work within the church.

3. **Elder:** this word was used to describe the same person while stressing his maturity and experience.

Within the same sentence you could have all three of these words but they would be referring to the same men (e.g. **elders** exercising **oversight** in **pastoring** their flock).

As time went on these terms were given to different people with different levels of authority (e.g. Bishops were responsible for Pastors) and new titles as well as levels of authority were added (e.g. Archbishop, Cardinal, Pope). These were not based on the authority of Scripture and reflected the gradual falling away from the early church's practice of carefully following the Apostles' teaching on these matters.

During Peter the Apostle's ministry in the 1st century church, the terms Elder, Shepherd, Pastor, Overseer, Bishop and Presbyter were all words that described the character, authority and work of a church leader, not different types of leaders. Each congregation had more than one leader and their authority was always limited to the local congregation.

Peter counts himself among this group because aside from being an Apostle (one who had been called by Jesus and witnessed His baptism, death and resurrection), he also served as an elder in the church at Jerusalem. Based on his role as an inspired Apostle and experience as an elder, he teaches them how grace affects the service of those who lead in the church.

1. Shepherd Willingly

> ^{2a} shepherd the flock of God among you, exercising oversight not under compulsion, but voluntarily, according to the will of God;

He tells them to shepherd, feed and take care of the flock because this is their primary responsibility.

The flock belongs to the shepherds and they are responsible for the direction, the feeding and protection of that flock. They have help in doing this (deacons, preachers, teachers, saints), but it is their flock and they are the ones who will answer to God for the souls won or lost, not these others. In connection with this, he also says that they are to shepherd willingly, not grudgingly. It should be a work eagerly done, not something they have to be reminded of or pressured into.

Shepherding should also be done according to God's will, and, in the next verses, he describes what that should look like.

2. Shepherd for Spiritual Reasons

> ^{2b} and not for sordid gain, but with eagerness;

There are many reasons why some men would want to lead in the church:

- Prestige, pride
- Desire to exercise power
- Financial gain (especially those who preach and teach in leadership)

Peter says that grace motivates men to become elders because they are eager to give something, not gain something.

3. Shepherd by Example

> ³ nor yet as lording it over those allotted to your charge, but proving to be examples to the flock.

In the world, a promotion often means that your job is to organize and direct others to do the heavy lifting and the dirty work. In the church, becoming an elder means that a man takes on the responsibility of acting like Christ so that the others will know how Christ would act in a given situation. Elders exercise authority through teaching, encouragement and loving example, and are not to act like lords or kings.

4. Shepherd with Hope

> ⁴ And when the Chief Shepherd appears, you will receive the unfading crown of glory.

The work is demanding, but the reward is great because the elders will receive from the Supreme Shepherd the highest of honor. There is always discussion about degrees of rewards, but the book of Revelation describes the throne of God surrounded with elders first then the saints and angels.

Grace creates a leadership that is different from the world; a leadership that is in harmony, that eagerly wants to serve its charge without complaining, a leadership submitted to God, a leadership that leads by example and not by decree, and a leadership with its eyes fixed on a heavenly crown not a worldly one. This means that elders lead with hope and joy, not fear, doubt or negativeness.

Grace Means a Responsive Congregation

Leaders don't lead in a vacuum. You need the proper response from the congregation in order to have a successful, spiritual leadership. Peter explains that grace also affects how the church responds to godly, gracious leadership.

> 5a You younger men, likewise, be subject to your elders; and all of you, clothe yourselves with humility toward one another,

The younger men are to obey their leaders. Some may have ideas, agendas, talents, etc., but grace allows the strongest of men to fold their ambitions and talents into the direction of their elders in the church.

> 5b for "God is opposed to the proud, but gives grace to the humble."

Peter now repeats this to the entire congregation and adds that this humble attitude should not only be directed towards the elders, but should also be the way that everyone is treated in the church.

In the following verses (6-11) he gives three reasons why all of this is necessary (that elders lead properly, that men submit, that everyone should have a humble attitude towards one another).

1. God Loves Those Who Humble Themselves

> 6 Therefore humble yourselves under the mighty hand of God, that He may exalt you at the proper

> time, ⁷ casting all your anxiety on Him, because He cares for you.

When leaders rely on God for strength to lead; when the church trusts God to guide them through their leaders; when everyone relies on God rather than self, God will provide all that we need. Grace enables us to humble ourselves before God, our church leaders and one another.

2. The Devil is Looking for the Proud

> ⁸ Be of sober spirit, be on the alert. Your adversary, the devil, prowls around like a roaring lion, seeking someone to devour.

Humility in leadership and in the congregation is not a curse or a punishment, it is the way to avoid the devil who continually searches to destroy Christians and finds easy targets among those who are proud.

The great favor of grace is that it enables us to temper our pride and cultivates in us the humility necessary to avoid the schemes of the evil one.

3. This Attitude will be Rewarded

> ⁹ But resist him, firm in your faith, knowing that the same experiences of suffering are being accomplished by your brethren who are in the world. ¹⁰ After you have suffered for a little while, the God of all grace, who called you to His eternal glory in Christ, will Himself perfect, confirm, strengthen and establish you.

This is not an easy thing to maintain for leaders or followers. Some Christians in Peter's day were being martyred because of their faith, and humbly accepted their death without giving up hope. The reason for this is that God Himself was perfecting, assuring, strengthening and establishing them in the kind of faith necessary to accomplish this.

Peter says that God will do the same for all those who allow the grace of God to create a humble heart in them.

Praise, verse 11, Doxology (Spontaneous Praise)

> ¹¹ To Him be dominion forever and ever. Amen.

At the end of his teaching, Peter finishes with an expression of praise and reverence to God as he ponders the things just said.

Salutation

Letters in those days had the greeting at the end and this was no exception.

> ¹² Through Silvanus, our faithful brother (for so I regard him), I have written to you briefly, exhorting and testifying that this is the true grace of God. Stand firm in it!

The letter was probably delivered by Silvanus, and in this verse he gives the summary or theme of his entire epistle. This is what the grace of God is all about:

- Security
- Sobriety
- Submission
- Suffering
- Service

Remain firm in these ideas and practices.

> ¹³ She who is in Babylon, chosen together with you, sends you greetings, and so does my son, Mark.

The church in Rome (referred to as Babylon) and his disciple, along with the one who served as secretary, Mark (the gospel of Mark) send their greetings.

> ¹⁴ Greet one another with a kiss of love.

A final greeting and encouragement (men kissed men, women kissed women). Peace for those who are Christians.

Summary

Peter makes two important points about grace in this first letter:

1. The grace of God **saves** a person.
2. The grace of God **changes** a person.

The connection between these two is that if grace hasn't changed your life, it hasn't saved your soul. The salvation of your soul is witnessed by the change in your life.

CHAPTER 6
PETER'S LAST SERMON

II Peter 1:1-11

In his first letter, Peter explains the effects of grace on a person and how one can recognize the changes taking place because of it. In this, his second letter, Peter deals with different issues because his own situation was different. Imagine, for a moment, if you were the one that God had chosen to do the following things:

1. Preach the very first gospel sermon.

2. Organize and serve as an elder in the first congregation of the Lord's church.

3. Receive the opportunity to be first in bringing the gospel to the Gentiles.

4. Produce inspired writings.

5. Along with the other Apostles, provide leadership for all the churches throughout the then known world.

If you had all of these responsibilities, as Peter did, and you knew you were going to die soon, what would you do?

Historians tell us that Peter was in Rome in 67 AD and caught up in the persecution of Christians going on then. Some say he was finally executed by being crucified upside down. Whatever the manner of his death, he knew the end was near and managed to write one last letter to the churches before his execution. Peter had one last chance to speak to the brethren, one last sermon to give, one last opportunity to teach them, and this letter (II Peter) contains what the Holy Spirit directed him to write in this final communication.

Grow or Die

The first thing he wanted them to remember is the following: as Christians you must grow spiritually or you will die spiritually.

Peter reminds them that Christianity is a process, a journey, a transformation that must take place. In chapter 1:1-11 of his second epistle he describes the changes that need to take place, not only to complete the journey, but also to confirm that Christians are actually on the right road.

> [1] Simon Peter, a bond-servant and apostle of Jesus Christ,
> To those who have received a faith of the same kind as ours, by the righteousness of our God and Savior, Jesus Christ:

He begins by introducing himself and the relationship that he and his readers have.

He is an Apostle (special messenger) of Jesus Christ. There are many messengers (evangelists, missionaries), but only those who had been chosen by Jesus and witnessed both his baptism and resurrection could be referred to as Apostles (except Paul).

Apostles had a special calling (Jesus Himself); a special experience (been with Jesus throughout His ministry); a special task (witness of His resurrection through miracles); a special authority (their letters were inspired by God).

Note that he also uses the words "bond-servant" in referring to himself, a term that demonstrates his great humility before the Lord. Yes, he is a special Apostle with special gifts and authority, but all that this means is that he is a slave to Jesus Christ, not someone who lords his position over others.

Peter describes his readers as people who are basically the same as himself and the other Apostles, people who have been saved because of God's grace through faith in Jesus Christ. He may have a special role and responsibility in the church, but in essence, he is connected to them in the same way all Christians are connected to one another. All were sinners and had been saved through faith in Christ, made possible by God's kindness and righteousness.

In these next verses (2-4), Peter offers a blessing and then explains how we come into the blessing he offers.

> [2] Grace and peace be multiplied to you in the knowledge of God and of Jesus our Lord;

Grace is the word that encompasses all of the good things that God gives His people (favors). Peace is the feeling and condition that one who receives God's grace finds himself in. Peter says that this combination of blessings and the enjoyment that comes from them will increase in proportion to the degree that a person comes to know God and Jesus Christ His Son. This word "know" is not just a casual knowledge or acquaintance, it denotes an exact or full knowledge. The degree of knowledge where the known can influence the one who is known.

> [3] seeing that His divine power has granted to us everything pertaining to life and godliness, through the true knowledge of Him who called us by His own glory and excellence.

Humans can know God only to the degree that He reveals Himself. For example, we can know that God is creative, powerful and wise from what He has made. But the creation doesn't reveal what He thinks, what He wants from man, what the future will be or what the spiritual world is like. The knowledge of these things is only available if God actually reveals it to man. Man can only know God, and consequently experience the blessings and peace that come from knowing Him, to the degree that God allows Himself to be known. Jesus said that the essence of eternal life was, "…knowing God and His Son Jesus Christ" (John 17:3).

Concerning this, Peter says that God has opened Himself up to full disclosure because He has permitted "true knowledge," and this true knowledge was made available through the gospel (which he refers to as "the calling") and the appearance of Jesus Christ (who he refers to as "His own glory and excellence").

What Peter is saying here is that the life and godliness that come with true knowledge of God is now available because God has fully revealed Himself through Jesus Christ. So, if grace and peace increase as I know God, there is good news: God is open to be known fully!

In verse 4, he summarizes and explains the true nature of the blessings and peace that he first mentioned in verse 2.

> [4] For by these He has granted to us His precious and magnificent promises, so that by them you may become partakers of the divine nature, having escaped the corruption that is in the world by lust.

Through the revelation of Himself God, has given us true knowledge. True knowledge gives us access to godliness and spiritual life. These blessings enable us to escape the condemnation that will fall on those who remain ignorant of God, corrupted by sin and attached to this world (we are not here to save the earth, we are here to call man to come out of this perishing world). In other words, knowing God and Christ is a great blessing because this knowledge permits us to escape the destruction that will come to this world and all those who are part of it.

In the next seven verses (5-11), Peter explains how this knowledge of God and Christ is developed. It is a cooperative effort involving God, Christ and the individual. Here's how it works:

1. God creates the universe and man, and then sets all into motion. There is perfect harmony between God, man and the creation until man sins. Because of disobedience, man loses his knowledge of and relationship with God, and is doomed to suffer and die along with the physical world.

2. Christ comes to earth in order to atone for man's sins, enable man to once again know and have a relationship with God, and save himself from the decay and death that the world is suffering.

3. Man responds to God by believing in Christ and thus receives back the knowledge and relationship he forfeited because of sin. He can now look forward to an eternal life with God in the new heavens and earth that God has prepared for all believers.

In verses 5-11, Peter describes man's part in knowing God, and how this affects his life and salvation. He explains the growth process that leads to an ever increasing knowledge of God.

> [5] Now for this very reason also, applying all diligence, in your faith supply moral excellence, and in your moral excellence, knowledge, [6] and in your knowledge, self-control, and in your self-control, perseverance, and in your perseverance, godliness, [7] and in your godliness, brotherly kindness, and in your brotherly kindness, love.

Peter says that the process begins with diligence, effort, commitment and resolve to the process itself. You cannot know God if you are lukewarm about it.

> And without faith it is impossible to please Him, for he who comes to God must believe that He is and that He is a rewarder of those who seek Him.
> - Hebrews 11:6

After establishing the attitude, Peter lists seven pairs of virtues, that when pursued, lead us to a fuller knowledge of God that in turn produces peace and joy within us:

1. **Faith and moral excellence** — The process begins with believing in God and what He says. This is naturally followed by doing what He says. A person's faith grows and is confirmed when he begins to live according to what he believes.

2. **Moral excellence and knowledge** — To a good and pure life one is to add knowledge (this is not knowledge of God, a different word is used here). This

knowledge is information, wisdom, the knowledge of oneself, one's world and God's Word. Peter is not only talking about the ability to be a good person, but the ability to apply God's Word to all situations in life. This requires knowledge and maturity.

3. **Knowledge and self-control** — A wise person becomes a prudent person. A knowledgeable person begins to understand the nature of the enemy and his strength. A knowing person understands that controlling one's self, controlling one's tongue, controlling one's thoughts, are the surest way to maintain faith and moral excellence.

4. **Self-control and perseverance** — Once the ABC's of the Christian walk are learned (faith in God, holy living, knowledge, self-control), the key is to continue in these things regardless of what happens. Many learn about the faith, are happy to get rid of the sins that destroyed their lives in the first place, and love to know more about God, but when adversity, persecution, pain or inconvenience comes, they give up and fall away. Peter says that it is important to cultivate the ability to persevere in things already learned, habits already acquired.

5. **Perseverance and godliness** — This is the point in the transformation that the new self becomes more evident. Many people, for various reasons of training, idealism or self-will, are wise, prudent and perseverant, but only those who develop these qualities in a Christian context begin to evidence godliness in their lives. I refer to this point in Christian development as "spiritual lift-off." It is similar to a plane taking off. For a time on the runway a plane is moving but still on the ground. At a certain speed, however, the wheels leave the ground and the plane takes flight..."lift-off." In many ways Christians, as they begin their walk with Christ, look pretty much like everyone

else around them. They are still moving on the ground so to speak. But as they grow in the process that Peter is explaining, they eventually begin cultivating the virtue of godliness, and it is at this point that they experience "spiritual lift-off." Godliness means to be more like God than to be like man; to be more like Jesus than to be like yourself; to belong more to the church than to belong to this world. The regeneration process is definitely beginning to show outwardly at this point. This is spiritual "lift off."

6. **Godliness and brotherly kindness** — Jesus said that the unmistakable sign of discipleship was the love that one disciple had for other disciples (John 13:35). The one who knows God understands that God sent Jesus to die in order to establish the church. God loves the church and those who know God, also love the church. For God, the church is the most important thing. Not to love the church, to disparage the church, to ignore or minimize the importance of the church, to be unfaithful to the church is a sign that one does not really know God very well. The head of the church is God the Son, Jesus Christ. To be godly is to be a lover of those who make up the church.

7. **Brotherly kindness and love** — Loving those who love the Lord is a sign that you know the Lord. Loving those who hate the Lord, hate you, hate the church is not only a sign that you know the Lord, it is a sign that you love in the way that He does as well. Our knowledge of God is only complete when we begin to love as He did, and are willing to lay down our lives for others, even others who hate us, like He did. Christian love is the sure sign that as long as it is possible in this weak flesh, our knowledge of God is complete and we are enjoying the blessings and peace that God gives to all those who love as He loved.

> ⁸ For if these qualities are yours and are increasing, they render you neither useless nor unfruitful in the true knowledge of our Lord Jesus Christ. ⁹ For he who lacks these qualities is blind or short-sighted, having forgotten his purification from his former sins.

Peter repeats his primary idea in these verses. The way to know God and enjoy the blessings of salvation is to continue growing or developing these virtues. To this he adds a second thought: ignoring these things or not concentrating on these things is foolish and a sign that a person is forgetting God's kindness in forgiving him in the first place.

Verses 10-11, a final word on encouragement:

> ¹⁰ Therefore, brethren, be all the more diligent to make certain about His calling and choosing you; for as long as you practice these things, you will never stumble; ¹¹ for in this way the entrance into the eternal kingdom of our Lord and Savior Jesus Christ will be abundantly supplied to you.

He repeats the original word "diligent." Make an effort, pay attention, stay focused on these things and several things will be produced:

…If you focus on these things…

1. You will feel sure, confident and secure about your salvation. There will be no guilt, fear of death or dread of judgment because you are certain that you will go to heaven. Knowledge of God brings greater security.

2. You will sin less and less. Sin causes trouble, sorrow, worry and pain. Those who are diligent in these things

will sin less and not lose faith which might cause one to fall away from Christ and sin more.

3. You will grow in your knowledge of God and His Son Jesus (this idea now described as entering the kingdom). The change we undergo is the process of being transported from earth to heaven, the final break coming at death.

Peter says that those who practice these virtues will experience an accelerated transfer from the earthly to the heavenly. They will begin to experience heaven before they are actually transported to heaven.

Summary

Of course, Peter was not simply philosophizing here or indulging in theological speculation. He was talking to real people about their spiritual lives and how to develop these. The practical application for our lives is to determine where we are at in the process. Are we at the beginning dealing with the preliminary issues of faith and morals, being baptized, giving up our bad habits, getting to church on a regular basis? Or, are we further along in the process, persevering in leadership, struggling to maintain a godly image in a perverse world?

Wherever we are at, this lesson is a reminder that:

1. We need to be diligent in our efforts to grow spiritually. It is not an easy process, however, it must be done because, as Peter teaches, if we don't grow, we die.

2. There is a pattern to this growth and Peter describes it here. We can know where we are at in the process.

3. The ultimate goal is to love like Jesus loved. God is love and to know Him is to know love.

CHAPTER 7
BEWARE OF FALSE TEACHERS

II Peter 1:12-2:22

Peter's second epistle is essentially this Apostle's last sermon to the church before his death. In it he makes several key exhortations about the Christian life. In the previous chapter we studied the first of these which was, "Grow or Die!" Christianity is a fluid experience of growth and development towards a goal. Once the growth stops, spiritual regression begins until our faith dies and along with it, our spiritual life.

In this second letter Peter explains that what fuels this growth is the on-going knowledge of God and Jesus Christ, a knowledge revealed in His Word and through His only begotten Son. Peter details how this knowledge of God is acquired on a daily basis. He explains the nuts and bolts of how a person gets to know God and how to continue in the process of spiritual development. Peter says that beginning with faith (which saves us) we are to add moral excellence, knowledge, self-control, perseverance, godliness, brotherly kindness and love. He concludes that the person who is practicing these things will grow in his knowledge of God, grow in his confidence of salvation, and grow in his appreciation and experience of the heavenly kingdom where he will eventually dwell forever.

Peter now turns from a discussion about things in the future in order to talk about two things that concern them in the here and now.

The Inspiration of God's Word

The process that ultimately leads to heaven begins with faith, a faith that is generated by hearing God's Word (Romans 10:17). Since the Word is the source of faith, Peter wants to reassure them that the basis for their faith and spiritual growth is sure.

> [12] Therefore, I will always be ready to remind you of these things, even though you already know them, and have been established in the truth which is present with you. [13] I consider it right, as long as I am in this earthly dwelling, to stir you up by way of reminder, [14] knowing that the laying aside of my earthly dwelling is imminent, as also our Lord Jesus Christ has made clear to me.

He confirms that what he has taught them are not new ideas. They are teachings that have been taught and known through the gospel (truth) which began the process in them in the first place. Peter finds it necessary, however, to remind them of this truth one last time because the Lord has revealed to him that he is about to die.

> [15] And I will also be diligent that at any time after my departure you will be able to call these things to mind. [16] For we did not follow cleverly devised tales when we made known to you the power and coming of our Lord Jesus Christ, but we were eyewitnesses of His majesty. [17] For when He received honor and glory from God the Father, such an utterance as this was made to Him by the Majestic Glory, "This is My beloved Son with whom I am well-pleased"— [18] and we ourselves heard this utterance made from heaven when we were with Him on the holy mountain.

This letter will serve as a constant reminder to them after he is gone. He tells them why his letter, along with the other Apostolic writings and Scriptures they have in their possession, should be considered inspired and authoritative.

1. The Apostles did not create the gospel. They were eyewitnesses of Jesus' baptism, ministry of teaching and miracles as well as His death and resurrection. Their preaching was not made up of fables and stories, but an eyewitness account of the life, death and resurrection of the Son of God.

2. In addition to this, they were also witnesses to His relationship to the Father in heaven, having seen both the glory of heaven (in Christ's transfigured state) and also heard it as God spoke from heaven (Matthew 17:1-9).

> [19] So we have the prophetic word made more sure, to which you do well to pay attention as to a lamp

> shining in a dark place, until the day dawns and the morning star arises in your hearts.

The Apostles not only had the words of the prophets describing the coming of the Messiah and what He would do, they also witnessed His coming and fulfillment of all the prophecies about Him. Therefore, the brethren would do well to pay attention to the things written by them for their spiritual development.

> [20] But know this first of all, that no prophecy of Scripture is a matter of one's own interpretation, [21] for no prophecy was ever made by an act of human will, but men moved by the Holy Spirit spoke from God.

The prophets did not speak from themselves, but were inspired as to what they would say by the Holy Spirit.

- The word inspired means "God breathed."

- The image of this word in the Greek language is that of a sail boat moved by the wind. There can be many styles of sailboats, but the one thing they have in common is that it is the wind that moves them along.

- Different men in different times wrote the Bible, but the one thing in common was that each was moved by the Holy Spirit to write what he wrote.

The point Peter is making here is that even though he and the other Apostles witnessed the life and teaching of Christ, it was by the power of the Holy Spirit that they and he wrote to the churches. His readers can have confidence, even after he is gone, in his words because they are not his words, they are words guided by the Holy Spirit of God. Essentially, Peter is claiming that his writings are inspired.

Since the Word is the source of faith, foundation for growth and entry into the kingdom of heaven, it will be a special target for Satan to destroy. One of his attacks will be to imbed false teachers within the church.

> [1] But false prophets also arose among the people, just as there will also be false teachers among you, who will secretly introduce destructive heresies, even denying the Master who bought them, bringing swift destruction upon themselves. [2] Many will follow their sensuality, and because of them the way of the truth will be maligned; [3] and in their greed they will exploit you with false words; their judgment from long ago is not idle, and their destruction is not asleep.

The nation of Israel had false prophets who tried to lure the people into idolatry or merely served evil kings for favor. Peter cautions that in the same way, lying teachers will come into the church to introduce false doctrines, even denying that Christ is God! He says that the penalty for false prophets in the future, as it was in the past in Israel, will be swift destruction. The false teachers may be on the earth for a while, but when judgment comes their destruction will be sudden and final.

Unfortunately, many will be taken in by false teaching and teachers. These will be led into disbelief and the life of sinfulness that disbelief breeds, as well as manipulation and swindling that often accompanies false religious teachers. Peter says that their success does not cancel or mask the certain judgment that is awaiting them.

> [4] For if God did not spare angels when they sinned,

> but cast them into hell and committed them to pits of darkness, reserved for judgment; ⁵ and did not spare the ancient world, but preserved Noah, a preacher of righteousness, with seven others, when He brought a flood upon the world of the ungodly; ⁶ and if He condemned the cities of Sodom and Gomorrah to destruction by reducing them to ashes, having made them an example to those who would live ungodly lives thereafter;

Speaking of judgment, he mentions those who were judged in the past, as a reminder to those who thought that judgment for these people was slow or not coming at all.

1. Angels were judged and punished for leaving their position and aspiring to be greater than God or not under His rule.

2. The ancient world was wiped out by a flood for its wickedness.

3. Sodom and Gomorrah were destroyed for their sins as well.

If they doubt judgment and punishment in the future, they should look at the past and see what God did to the wicked then, for these were punished as an example for future generations.

> ⁷ and if He rescued righteous Lot, oppressed by the sensual conduct of unprincipled men ⁸ (for by what he saw and heard that righteous man, while living among them, felt his righteous soul tormented day after day by their lawless deeds), ⁹ then the Lord knows how to rescue the godly from temptation, and to keep the unrighteous under punishment for the day of judgment,

Peter declares that God not only knows how to punish, He also knows how to save.

God deals with both the obedient and the disobedient in times of evil and temptation. For example:

- Lot was surrounded by evil but with God's help was able to resist the pressure and was ultimately saved from destruction.

- The others around him disobeyed and were destroyed.

The point here for the readers is that even though they may have to face false teachers and various trials of persecution on account of their faith, the same God who has the power to punish the evil ones also has the power to sustain them through their trials. Of course, he has already mentioned the way to be sustained in trial: to diligently add to faith moral excellence, to moral excellence knowledge, etc. Keep practicing the spiritual disciplines that develop your knowledge of God.

In verses 10-22, Peter finishes this chapter with a long description of the character, actions and attitude of the false teachers that have always and will always continue to plague God's church until Jesus returns.

> [10] and especially those who indulge the flesh in its corrupt desires and despise authority. Daring, self-willed, they do not tremble when they revile angelic majesties, [11] whereas angels who are greater in might and power do not bring a reviling judgment against them before the Lord.

They are sensual (carnal in nature, worldly) and hate authority (human or otherwise). They revile or blaspheme spiritual things without fear or shame. They teach falsely or ridicule spiritual things without regard.

Peter says that angels, who could destroy these people in an instant, do not even utter a word against them because judgment belongs to the Lord.

> [12] But these, like unreasoning animals, born as creatures of instinct to be captured and killed, reviling where they have no knowledge, will in the destruction of those creatures also be destroyed, [13a] suffering wrong as the wages of doing wrong. They count it a pleasure to revel in the daytime.

They are like animals who ravage and destroy on instinct but are doomed to be destroyed like the rabid creatures that they are.

> [13b] They are stains and blemishes, reveling in their deceptions, as they carouse with you, [14] having eyes full of adultery that never cease from sin, enticing unstable souls, having a heart trained in greed, accursed children;

These people are not confused, they know what they are doing and are enjoying it. They enjoy their sensual sins. They enjoy seducing unstable (immature) Christians, and they enjoy luring them into similar sins of greed and sexual immorality. He compares them to scabs and blemishes on the fellowship of true believers. Their constant motivation is sin and they have no conscience about destroying a person's faith or that of an entire congregation.

> ¹⁵ forsaking the right way, they have gone astray, having followed the way of Balaam, the son of Beor, who loved the wages of unrighteousness; ¹⁶ but he received a rebuke for his own transgression, for a mute donkey, speaking with a voice of a man, restrained the madness of the prophet.

Peter compares them to a prophet who was enticed by money to curse God's people but was stopped by an angel and the miraculous speaking of his own animal. His greed, however, overcame him on another occasion and he died a miserable death for having perverted his gift of prophesy (Numbers 31:8).

> ¹⁷ These are springs without water and mists driven by a storm, for whom the black darkness has been reserved.

Here he pronounces the final end of all such false prophets, past, present and future.

> ¹⁸ For speaking out arrogant words of vanity they entice by fleshly desires, by sensuality, those who barely escape from the ones who live in error, ¹⁹ promising them freedom while they themselves are slaves of corruption; for by what a man is overcome, by this he is enslaved.

Peter explains what some of the false teachers were doing at the time of his writing. They were telling new converts (the ones who had barely escaped) that they could be good Christians and still enjoy the sinful pleasures of their former lives outside of Christ. The result was that those without knowledge and self-control would go back to the things that they were enslaved to before being rescued by Christ. The false teachers were promoting their ideas with seductive preaching and high minded words that seemed intelligent. Some think that they were promoting, among other things, the Greek notion of Dualism. This philosophical idea taught that the flesh and spirit were separate entities and what a person did in one did not affect what happened in the other.

Of course, if you bought into this you could have it both ways; sin without guilt in the spirit, and worship without changing the flesh. This was false freedom, Peter said, because sin did not set one free, it imprisoned. One simply had to observe those imprisoned by alcohol, pornography, violence, greed and selfishness to see the falseness of this idea.

> [20] For if, after they have escaped the defilements of the world by the knowledge of the Lord and Savior Jesus Christ, they are again entangled in them and are overcome, the last state has become worse for them than the first. [21] For it would be better for them not to have known the way of righteousness, than having known it, to turn away from the holy commandment handed on to them. [22] It has happened to them according to the true proverb, "A dog returns to its own vomit," and, "A sow, after washing, returns to wallowing in the mire."

Here Peter rebukes not only the false teachers but the poor victims who are taken in by their hypocrisy and doctrines. He says three things to them:

1. If they go back to the world after having known Jesus and salvation, their second enslavement to sin will be worse than their first. This time their suffering will be accompanied by the awful realization that they had escaped this once before and put themselves right back into the same prison by their own hand.

2. It would be better for them to remain in ignorance because judgment will be worse for those who know better but disobey nevertheless.

3. Those who do this are not worthy of Christ, acting more like dumb animals than spiritual people.

In his warning, Peter points to the false teachers and reveals that they will be punished along with those who allow themselves to be seduced by them.

Summary

These admonitions were written 2000 years ago, but as Peter says, were meant to be relevant to us today because the words are inspired by God. From these writings we can draw a few warnings that would do us well to heed today:

1. Stick to the Word

Every heresy, every division, every apostasy always begins with the disrespect, disobedience or disbelief of God's inspired Word. So long as the Bible in its entirety remains the sole authority and teacher, we will always have a lamp to guide our feet through this dark world. We don't always agree about what it says or how to do things (that's normal), but we must always agree that it is God's Word and our search begins and ends there.

2. Beware of False Teachers

They come in all shapes and sizes.

- Some are obvious, who use religion as a cloak to gain political or social power, wealth and prestige.

- Some are like moles who spread their false ideas one person at a time in the congregation.

One of the primary tasks of elders (Acts 20) is to monitor and guard against false teaching and teachers in the church. The Bible even tells us what to do with false teachers:

> [17] Now I urge you, brethren, keep your eye on those who cause dissensions and hindrances contrary to the teaching which you learned, and turn away from them. [18] For such men are slaves, not of our Lord Christ but of their own appetites; and by their smooth and flattering speech they deceive the hearts of the unsuspecting.
> - Romans 16:17-18

Watch or identify who they are and turn away or disfellowship them.

A false teacher, however, is not someone who may have a different opinion as you do on some Bible topic. Paul and Peter list the types of things that identify one as a false teacher:

1. A lifestyle contrary to the teaching of Christ. Someone who says one thing and does another.

2. An attempt to draw one away from holy and pure living.

3. Teachings and actions that create strife and division in the church.

4. Teaching that denies the deity of Christ and tries to change God's plan for salvation (e.g. salvation by works or rituals rather than by faith in Christ expressed in repentance and baptism).

Peter says that these types are always preying on the church and we must beware of them.

3. God will Punish Evil and Disbelief

The tragedy of false teachers is that not only will they be punished by God for their sins of greed and lying, etc., but so will the poor victims who were led astray by their false teachings and examples. The crown of eternal life goes to the one who remains faithful until the end. Peter says that seduction by a false teacher is no excuse for falling away. For example:

- Leaving the church to join a movement and then becoming disillusioned with religion and quitting altogether.

- Becoming discouraged and falling away because of the sins of a church leader.

- Leaving the church because it seemed that members were hypocrites or someone offended us.

False teachers are dangerous, but they are not a legitimate excuse for being unfaithful to Christ and His church.

84

CHAPTER 8
DON'T WORRY BE READY

II Peter 3:1-18

Peter is writing what is to be his last sermon to the churches. In this letter, he reviews some key ideas that he hopes they will remember and practice after he is gone. While they were alive, the Apostles were the source of God's Word for Christians. In a way they were living, breathing Bibles. After their death, however, the church was left with God's Word in written form to provide the way of salvation, growth and encouragement.

Peter's letter summarizes what Christians need to observe if they wish to remain faithful to Christ and thus guarantee their entry into heaven. So far we've studied three important teachings that Peter left for the disciples of Jesus to understand and practice:

1. You must continue to grow and develop as a Christian or you will die spiritually

This, he said, is accomplished by deliberately cultivating the Christian virtues of knowledge, purity, self-control, patience, kindness and love. He doesn't explain how to do this, just that they needed to do this in order to grow. We know that Christian virtues are cultivated through obedience to the Word, service to others, prayer and praise to God, evangelism, study and fellowship. These are the things that we, as members of the church, participate in and practice week in and week out. The purpose of "church life" is to cultivate the very things that Peter talks about so we can continue our growth and thus assure our entry into heaven. If we understood how local church life fits into the "big picture" of Christian development that Peter describes in his letters, we would be motivated to make a greater effort to follow his instructions.

Christian life is not just about coming to church or fixing a meal for a person who is sick or avoiding bad habits. These are the exercises that help develop the spiritual growth necessary for knowing God in this life, and guaranteeing our transfer into the next life when Jesus returns to bring all the faithful to be with Him in heaven eternally.

2. The Scriptures are inspired

Peter encouraged his readers to remain faithful to God's Word. He was addressing two groups who needed convincing of this:

- Jews who had become Christians considered the "Scriptures" to be what Moses and the prophets had written.

- Gentiles who had become Christians had no "Scriptures" as part of their former religious experience.

Peter reminds them that he and the other Apostles had actually seen the miracles, the resurrection of Jesus and had actually heard words spoken by God Himself:

- For the Jews, this meant that God was now speaking through Jesus and His Apostles who provided written records of Jesus' teachings.

- For the Gentiles, the fact that God spoke through these Apostles was a new phenomenon confirmed by powerful signs.

Peter instructs both groups that a new standard had been established through himself and the other Apostles. A standard and authority that superseded Moses and the prophets for the Jews, and the content of the former pagan religions practiced by the Gentiles.

The new standard was God's Word contained in the Apostolic writings. This was to be their guide from now on.

3. Be careful of false teachers

Because the church had been led exclusively by inspired teachers relaying God's Word to them, they would be especially vulnerable to uninspired teachers who would come in and preach false doctrine to them. While the Apostles were alive, they could discern who was true from who was fake, but now they had to be careful to compare and judge their teachers and their teachings according to:

- The accuracy of their teaching in comparison to the Scriptures

- Obvious discrepancies between their lifestyle and their teaching
- The presence of spiritual motivation or worldly motivation

This was important because God would not only punish the false teachers, but would also punish those who became unfaithful to the Lord because of false teachers. In the last chapter, Peter provides them with a final word of advice and encouragement.

Don't Be Discouraged, Be Ready - Chapter 3

These Christians lived at a time when Christianity was being publicly persecuted and their leaders were being jailed and executed. In addition to this, there were false teachers infiltrating the church and trying to destroy it from within. In response to these problems Peter says, "Don't be discouraged, be ready." As far as Peter was concerned, being ready meant two things:

1. Being Faithful Until the End

Their detractors mocked these Christians' hope of Jesus' return, but Peter encourages them not to lose the hope of His coming again at the end of the world.

> [1] This is now, beloved, the second letter I am writing to you in which I am stirring up your sincere mind by way of reminder, [2] that you should remember the words spoken beforehand by the holy prophets and the commandment of the Lord and Savior spoken by your apostles.

He himself has written twice to encourage and motivate them by remembering what the prophets and Jesus (through the Apostles) have told them. The "commandment" that they all spoke of was to remain faithful. The prophets continually reminded the Israelites to remain true to God and not fall into idolatry (this was the first of the Ten Commandments). In the same way, Jesus told His disciples that they needed to be faithful until the end in order to receive the crown (Matthew 10:22).

> [3] Know this first of all, that in the last days mockers will come with their mocking, following after their own lusts, [4] and saying, "Where is the promise of His coming? For ever since the fathers fell asleep, all continues just as it was from the beginning of creation." [5] For when they maintain this, it escapes their notice that by the word of God the heavens existed long ago and the earth was formed out of water and by water, [6] through which the world at that time was destroyed, being flooded with water. [7] But by His word the present heavens and earth are being reserved for fire, kept for the day of judgment and destruction of ungodly men.

He tells them not to be discouraged on account of the persecution they suffered because of their beliefs. Some mocked their belief in the return of Jesus and the end of the world. Those who did this, however, forgot that at one time others mocked Noah as he prepared for the end of life on earth, and at God's Word the great flood came and destroyed them all. He continues to say that by God's Word there will once again be the destruction of heaven and earth. However, this time it will be destroyed by intense heat. The judgment promised by God ultimately came to pass during Noah's time, and just as certainly the final judgment will come again when Jesus returns. This is certain because God has said so.

> ⁸ But do not let this one fact escape your notice, beloved, that with the Lord one day is like a thousand years, and a thousand years like one day. ⁹ The Lord is not slow about His promise, as some count slowness, but is patient toward you, not wishing for any to perish but for all to come to repentance.

Here Peter is providing an answer to those who challenge them by saying that the return of Christ (and by implication His resurrection) is not true because nothing is happening. In many cases people today think this as well. They point to the evil, injustice, illness and tragedy in the world, and say that if a loving God existed, He would not let these things happen. They reason that this must mean that God is not there or if He is, He doesn't care or His promise of justice and relief are not true.

Peter says two things about this:

1. God's time frame is different from ours. He is eternal, we are temporal. Taking ten human years or one hundred human years to accomplish His purpose seems like a lot to us but is inconsequential to Him. Everything God does is with an eternal (i.e. the number 1000 represents eternity) view and purpose, and so it is difficult for us who live a mere century at most to understand or imagine all that He plans or does. Much of what we do now may only bear fruit in one hundred or five hundred years. Only God knows the time frame and final purpose. This is why we must live and serve by faith.

2. God is patient and the slowness of judgment is not out of indifference but out of love. God is willing to wait decades for repentance because He knows that the punishment will be eternal, and He doesn't want anyone to suffer eternally. Only a fool, however, will

tempt God and make Him wait when he knows what he has to do.

> [10] But the day of the Lord will come like a thief, in which the heavens will pass away with a roar and the elements will be destroyed with intense heat, and the earth and its works will be burned up.

The recipients of Peter's letters are not to doubt that with time (God's own good time) the judgement will come and when it does, it will be:

- Sudden (no chance for repentance)

- Complete (everything will be destroyed by intense heat)

> [11] Since all these things are to be destroyed in this way, what sort of people ought you to be in holy conduct and godliness, [12] looking for and hastening the coming of the day of God, because of which the heavens will be destroyed by burning, and the elements will melt with intense heat! [13] But according to His promise we are looking for new heavens and a new earth, in which righteousness dwells.

Here Peter repeats his original exhortation by reminding them that since these things will happen, they should be faithful. Their faithfulness was demonstrated in holy conduct and godly character. Unlike the mockers and sinners, they should look forward to it (hasten doesn't mean that they can make it happen faster, it means be eager or anticipate this time). For disbelievers, sinners and the unfaithful, it will be a time of complete and terrible destruction, but for Christians it will mean a new beginning.

The old sinful world will be done away with and a new dimension or world that is in complete harmony with God will merge. God will reign with Christ and the Holy Spirit, and all those who are there will be equipped with glorified bodies that will be able to stand in the presence of God without fear or shame forever.

If these things are so, Peter's first admonition is that they should be ready by living faithfully until the end.

Being ready also meant...

2. Being Fruitful Until the End

You cannot be faithful unless you are fruitful. This was the idea he began with and ends with here. The way to remain faithful until the end is not just to wait until the end, but to grow until the end.

> [14] Therefore, beloved, since you look for these things, be diligent to be found by Him in peace, spotless and blameless, [15a] and regard the patience of our Lord as salvation;

Since they look forward to the end, they should therefore cultivate the qualities that will guarantee this outcome. Note: the word "diligent" again. You have to work at it:

- To be at peace with God and men
- To live in a pure and holy way

Not to give in to doubters and mockers, but to accept God's timetable and slowness of coming as an opportunity for salvation, not indifference.

> [15b] just as also our beloved brother Paul, according to the wisdom given him, wrote to you, [16] as also in all his letters, speaking in them of these things, in which are some things hard to understand, which the untaught and unstable distort, as they do also the rest of the Scriptures, to their own destruction. [17] You therefore, beloved, knowing this beforehand, be on your guard so that you are not carried away by the error of unprincipled men and fall from your own steadfastness, [18] but grow in the grace and knowledge of our Lord and Savior Jesus Christ. To Him be the glory, both now and to the day of eternity. Amen.

These same things (that Peter writes to them about) have also been written about by Paul the Apostle. Peter encourages them to accept Paul's writings as authoritative and not be seduced by the false teachers who not only teach false doctrine, but also pervert the teachings of the Apostles. Being fruitful means growing in this kind of knowledge and the grace of the Lord.

Growth in the knowledge of God and His blessings guarantees a successful life as a Christian here on earth and entry into the new heavens and earth that God has promised.

Summary

Peter finishes his last sermon to an embattled church with a clear call to face opposition by being ready, not being discouraged. For Christians, then and now, being ready means two things: being faithful and being fruitful. 2000 years have gone by and still the Lord has not come:

- There are injustices and tragedies

- Sinners are bold in their practices

- Christianity is once again being discarded, mocked and even persecuted

And what shall our response be?

- We must be faithful with the attitude that, even if it takes 10,000 more years for Jesus to come, God is in charge and we are prepared to wait our entire lives and beyond.

- We must be fruitful in patience, knowledge, holy living, perseverance, godliness, kindness and love in order to maintain our faith until the end, and help others find faith so that they can be saved.

Have you become discouraged, unfaithful or unfruitful? Remember the warnings of God and be encouraged by His sure promises.

ALSO AVAILABLE FROM BIBLETALK BOOKS

- Understanding Your Religion: 7 Major Doctrines That Define Christianity
- The King and His Kingdom: Jesus in the Gospel of Matthew
- Lessons from the Kings: Ancient Wisdom for Modern Times
- In Love for Life: Building or Rebuilding a Great Marriage
- Top Ten Sins & Struggles
- Gospel of John: Jesus the God/Man
- Elders Deacons Preachers Saints
- 1st and 2nd Thessalonians: Preparing for the Second Coming
- Christianity for Beginners
- The Kingdom Parables
- Daniel / Revelation for Beginners
- Colossians for Beginners

BibleTalk.tv is an Internet Mission Work.

We provide textual Bible teaching material on our website and mobile apps for free. We enable churches and individuals all over the world to have access to high quality Bible materials for personal growth, group study or for teaching in their classes.

The goal of this mission work is to spread the gospel to the greatest number of people using the latest technology available. For the first time in history it is becoming possible to preach the gospel to the entire world at once. BibleTalk.tv is an effort to preach the gospel to all nations every day until Jesus returns.

The Choctaw Church of Christ in Oklahoma City is the sponsoring congregation for this work and provides the oversight for the BibleTalk ministry team. If you would like information on how you can support this ministry, please go to the link provided below.

---

bibletalk.tv/support

Made in the USA
Middletown, DE
22 March 2023